Moonlight Whispers

☾ Hadil Ahmed ☽

For Him
Who Stole My Heart

love comes in phases
just like words come in pages

The Symphony Of Love

☾

 in love we fly and fall, smile and cry, find and lose, get attached
and be broken… but one thing about love: it's beautiful, and that
beauty lies in the very depths.
it's an ocean where you can either dive or drown, a light that you can
either use to fill the shallow or let the darkness within you swallow,
a flower that you can either plant and watch it bloom or pick and let it
wilt.
love can be everything and anything you want it to be. it's the
celebration of life as it's the consolation for death. it's the proof of
happiness just as it is the testament of sadness.
and love is the innocence dipped in the sins. but despite all, it's still
beautiful.
i've been there, i've seen that beauty and embraced it within me.
the moon can tell you all about the secrets i whispered during the
night with a wish they will reach my beloved one through the
lasting light.

☽

Eclipse

Moonlight Whispers

☽

⟨

i called his name
couldn't be any more packed
with meanings than this
i attached it to all
the feelings that
ever resided my heart
and every thought that
more than once occupied my mind
it's so much weight to carry about
everywhere, everywhen
but i like to think that someday
i'll be as light as a feather
fluttering with the gentle winds

- Someday when i'm with him

it hurts like hell…
i want him but
cannot have him
not that he's not mine
but that a great distance
tears us apart
it feels like i'm right there
looking in his deep dreamy eyes
thirsting for his long warm hugs
but cannot touch him
...and it just hurts

☾

i've been tortured by your disappearance
for days that can't be counted in pages
i've been haunted by your shadow
for nights that can't be proven in words
i've loved you endless
i've missed you stopless
i've craved you limitless
still your absence goes on

on & on

☾

sometimes i wonder if he's just an illusion
i've built to warm up myself in this cold world
~ illusion

☾

he said that i shall promise to let go of him when i find someone better
and he forgot that i already have the best.
he said that i shall promise to look for someone who cares and loves me
and he forgot that no one would love me the way he does.
he said that i shall promise to always remember him when it's all over
and he forgot that i already carved his name in my heart.

☙ Forgotten Promise

☾

recently, every word he'd been saying is like a goodbye;
Brief*
Sad*
Ending*

(

he comes by night
and goes by day
i thought it was a pleasure
for him to torture me
but now i see it clear
i've loved dreams
so much i made up
a beautiful one
and named it
   "Him"

Dreamer

i'm so scared of losing you
after a long journey of
searching and waiting…
but i'm also scared of
falling too deep i can't
get up after…

❧ Loving you is a blessing
Loving you is a curse

☾

i've crossed the seas
chasing my dreams
i've erased the limits
within few minutes
but loving you is such a risk
i threw myself in
the deep shallow end
and hoped i can learn
how to swim before
i drown in

Shallow

((

i don't understand
what's going on in
that beautiful mind
behind those innocent eyes
and very decent looks

⤨ Something Pure

＜

i keep looking at
the door's entrance
growing dolorous
to see you coming
i've begun to worry
that it's taking you
too long to get here

Where have you been

_._._._._._._._._._._._.-

☾

i looked at the moon
in times he wasn't here
Sometimes
i was only able to see
the void laminate of it
Sometimes
i was only able to see
the dark forest on it
but barely in the middle
until there came a day i knew
the moon reflected what was within me

- When Everything Becomes Nothing
  And Nothing Becomes Everything

☾

i've loved him more than he would ever know
i've loved him more than i could ever absorb
could it be any more complicated

৩ Complicated

((

i didn't know anybody there
i only went for a fresh air
i know; loud music, crazy dancing
overflowing drinks, flirting giggles
and sexual actions are not
the kind of quiet walks one needs
but they are a resolve for a change
that definitely was a big change for me

i stayed standing in the corner
watching the show break
open on the dancefloor
then he approached me
a hazel-eyed stranger
i think i've come across before
once or twice in the school corridors
but i never knew him further

he started a nice conversation
that gradually evolved
into an unwelcome flirtation
and before i realized it
he was pushing closer
and i was stepping back
to the point i hit the wall
and captured his arms going up
tracing the wall and lastly
fixing on both sides across my head

i detected starvation in his dilating pupils
his hands began creeping up my face
so i could but turn my cheek to the side
and wish to disappear into the wallpaper
i had a scream in my throat
wanting to break free
but was blocked by the increasing stir

i closed my eyes
and wished on the darkness to rescue me
i felt a blow imposing
and a sudden pull steering me aside
bare hands held my corpse tight
then i felt safe but… how
since when queerness became safety
why am i trusting those hands to hold me
when i was eaten by fear from them
a measure of thousand heartbeats
in the last two minutes

it was you
you were there looking at me
face painted with worry
and livid voice growing softer
your hands climbed up all the way
from my waist to my cheeks
it's not safe for you here alone
what if anything happened to you
what if they hurt you? Are you alright?
do you ever think of anybody but yourself

i stared at the diminishing blueness of your eyes
searching for a response to questions i never picked
the-once-was fear decomposed into bewilderment
and sprouted into stupefaction
you hugged me and it all evaporated away

Friday Night

☾

... so whenever i longed for you
i looked to the sky and remembered
that we see the same
     M ○●N

☾

i was fine until
your love hit the
pivot of my heart
like the arrow
coming from a
gracious bow

⇻ Stories Untold:
Bow & Arrow

but if loving you means that
i will always be a prisoner
deprived of freedom and control
then i wish i never get to see
the outside world ever again

-   The Crime Of Loving You

☾

i wrote about you
until no ink is left
so i used my blood
instead hoping
feelings for and
thoughts of you
will be attached
are they still there
can you see them
do my words mean
something to you

♭ Pieces of Me

☾

i miss him
during daylight
i miss him
every dark night
and in the space
    between

    -    Twilight -

☾

breaking up   breaking down
i'm tired of taking the same old vertical way
i want something horizontal
something sempiternal

☣ Casualties

☾

no… but the truth that
my heart is ready to
cross the borders for you
frightens the hell out of me
what if i get lost
somewhere i've never been
and can't find my way back home

 a heart overseas

(

i've complained to my pen
about missing you
so many times
that the ink putrefied
from the sorrow
how can i bring it
back to life
how can i convince
my perishing heart
that every withering flower
can and will arise again
from the seed rooting
in the fertile ground
to the sphere where
care can be found

Fading Faith

☾

i'm not sure
if i want to do
this anymore
it's tearing me apart
every time we mess up

ঙ Latter Wreck

☾

flowers, roses and lilies
have started to bloom
i look at them with
the eyes of mere jealousy
as my heart yearns for
its abundant spring season
to come about well-nigh
what you have done to me ?
i keep digging for the sunlight
to shine through the dark side
and care for my wilting heart
but all i see is storms all around

❖   Herein

☾

i was never a beggar
but if i had to
i'd literally
desperately
beg you to
stay

{ For That's How Much You Mean To Me }

☾

days are getting longer
nights are becoming colder
moments growing harder
as i wait for you to step in
my humble world
it makes me wonder
if the visions that
have been in my head
would simulate the actuality
if the way you fantasized
is similar to the real self
that lives inside me
it has me holding my breath
on the tune of pendulum

⏲ Lunar Clock

☾

bitter silence
ultimate missing
light sleep
lovely agony
extreme loneliness
thorough confusion
•••
these feelings i have
for you quite often
they hurt
please
i'm begging you
make them go away

● Accurate Bullet

and if i could wave
a magical wand
and make anything
come true
i'd wish him to be
asleep in my arms
wrapped in a blanket
of my divine love
and i'd gaze at his
beautiful face
all night long
and be grateful
for that bliss
all life long

Fairy Dust

☾

we used to make
memories together
now you're just
another one of them

✦ Silver Jar

so aren't we warriors
when we fight the distance
when we challenge the barriers
when we stand against the universe
to be together, forever
and aren't we warriors
when we live a daily battle
defending our love story
so it gets to see the light
or when we hold each other tight
as everyone is trying to break us apart
aren't we warriors after all

ೞ Warriors

☾

i wish he ever
understands
that the cost
of loving him
was just too
expensive

$ Standard Price

☾

but the fair winds singing in my ear
remind me of your serene voice
the balmy waves of a deep blue sea
remind me of your pretty eyes
the cozy blankets covering my body
remind me of your warm hugs
the blossoming flowers surrounding my feet
remind me of your chaste touch
the light snowflakes landing on my cheeks
remind me of your soft kisses
the bright sunset of a midsummer day
reminds me of your alluring smile
the falling leaves of a late autumn sky
remind me of the destined day i fell for you
the sun, the moon, the stars....
everything somehow reminds me of you

⁊ Subtle Reminders

☾

every night i look at
the face of the moon
and wish it was yours

≈ Flirting with the Moon

☾

and i'll be there darling
when the waves crush by
holding echo of the days
we spent by the ocean
together

︵ Journals of a Replica

☾

dancing under the moonlight
his hands on my waist
i followed him as he paced
the stars sprinkling in my hair
glimmered on the lake's surface
yet him …
the utmost of all the stars
wasn't there

-    Dancing with a Shadow

((

once you get in a war
you'll fuck death in every breath
and love is but another honeyed kind of war
a war between wanting to stay and wanting to shut the door

                                                              Waning

☾

let it hurt
until my body gets used to it
to the invincible taste of doubt
to the mere feeling of loneliness
and the sore umbra of ignorance
let it hurt so bad
i won't feel it anymore after
instead it becomes a pleasure

☧ The Cure

i'm sorry
i had to do it
i had to lie and leave
hurting myself seemed to be
easier for me than hurting you
i guess i was wrong after all
for you were wounded
and i was wrecked

◆   Eclipse

☾

you said that
some stories die so
that others would be born
but baby what if I never
wanted ours to be torn

↻ Restart

the most irony part
is that he's both
my hurter
and
healer
at once

PuZzLe

should he know that frequently lately
emotional waves rock me by quietly
then suddenly throw me into the depths
and i wake up terrified
the taste of his name
still stings on the tip of my tongue
like the honeyed piercing of a bee
i sit up in bed all petrified barring my hands
they shake their way up to my neck
and wipe off the sweat drowning me
in the gloomy ocean of contemplations
since the day he walked away.
i'd see the light of the moon
filtering through the curtains
tracing silver-tinted blue wires across the room
so i stretch my arms to reach them
and my heart stretches along seeking relief

☾ Insomnia

(

we've been living
in the adequate
reflection of
oblivion

\3 Oblivion

☾

i wonder when we're gone
if the souls that once
loved each other
under our identities
will find their alley
on the other side
guided by a moonish light
under which
we both walked and
they both winged
to the same heart
we all once shared

　　　　　　　　※　Valley of Ashes

☾

it's escalated quickly
i worried if you were alright
as you've been gone all night
it then shifted into a sadness
i'd revere if i knew next is madness
and that dark betraying suspicion
had me seeing every other bad vision
i hated those filtering feelings of mistrust
took my will with a blow should you know that i must
there came the crashing and soon neutrality that stopped time
when everything became nothing
and i became something
just because you weren't here

(Monster)

☾

so if i'm a moon lover
doesn't that also
make me
the lover
of
darkness

➤ Devotion

((

there are so many untold tangled stories
in the simplicity of his short talk

Deep Tones

☾

but i'm not surprised
you've always been
so skilled at it …
at fully attracting
me to you,
playing it elusive
maybe you are
elusive after all

◉ Elusive

☾

you claimed
all of me
but you only
took hold of
few pieces

✳   Shattering Glass

(

am i something to you
just like you are
everything
to me

. Fetish

((

i don' t know how
you sneaked into
my shielded heart
but please, please
do not leave now
it's worshipped you

❧   A Heart's Crush

☾

you can't have my body,
if you don't earn my heart.
they come in one package

※   Heritage

i'm still believing your casual lies
after everything we've been through before
i'm still enacting the same old mistakes
after everything i've come to endure

Never Learning

☾

Someday
you are
going to be
the death
of me

☙ Fatal Weapon

☾

how can i show you that i'm not them
i'm not someone who's able of
tricking you into being theirs
trying to make you a person you're not
opening up their bodies for a pleasure
they made your concept of tenderness
then giving out that same pleasure
to those you thought you trust
i'm not them
i'm just someone who's believed
in the magic of life and wished
to share it with whom you are
i can't give you the pleasure they mastered
but i can surely wrap you in true love forever

-   i'm not them

☾

i wish it's easy for me
to kick you out
as it was easy
to let you in
but no man who
earns a kingdom
where he finds the
mortal truth of sovereignty
is ready to give up his throne
straightforwardly
and baby your throne
lays in my heart

*R*eign

((

don't mind all the
given promises you broke
don't either mention any of
the bitter tears you caused to drop
i'm only asking for one thing instead
you always make me happy when i'm sad
can you comfort me now that i'm weeping

ॐ Hopeless Willow

☽

why do you keep giving me
those fake false hopes
when you already know
they never existed
never going to
why do you create
these things inside me
and leave me to figure
my way through them alone
when you know i already
have enough to deal with

/ Delusion

i want him to want me
but when he does
when he has all of me
i hesitate
" what if there
remains nothing else
to want after that …
nothing he hasn't heretofore
got to explore "
i think i enjoy being
a mystery he craves

∝   Ever Crave

☾

i had to get used
to blaming you
for walking away
rather than
torturing myself
for letting you go

☾ Guilt

☾

even when
you break my heart
and leave
i still look for a way
to win you back

℩Unaccountable

☾

stay
and when you leave
take my heart with
you

-   The Very Last Goodbye

☾

it's all your fault
you got me so deeply
attached to you
and now, my lover
you're censuring me
for missing you ?

≒   Bad Habits

☾

a birthstone formed
from moonlight
i swore to guard
and keep under sight
for a great tale
dwells within :
when the moon
appears full up high
and the blue sheen
dances inside
his love will find
its way to my heart
and eventually
rest its tender passion
in my carved chest

♣ Moonstone

((

i was alone in the dark
red-wine dress rubbing
against the black sand
of the fine beach
and a hair as dark
as the far horizon ahead
paddling with the salty winds
the sky was eclipsed
by a moon bleeding red
pouring vivid light like
the streaming lava of volcano
i felt the petals of a curse
smacking against my skeleton
as i ran to catch the ghost of you
slowly overlapping with
the dense murkiness fading
in a nightmare you were wading

" Bloody Moon

☾

do you ever miss me
like i always miss you

⇄ Simulation

you said you will
take care of me
but you lied
i'm hurting and
falling asleep crying
but you're somewhere
else than right here
to rescue me from the
phantoms in my room

-    Damn Liar

☾

you indulged my body
so often that
no minute passes
without it craving you
and my soul remains
the helpless victim
between you two

-    Shades of Coral

☾

how can i
love again
when
he took
my heart
with him
for good

- Thief

(

tonight i'll shower ;
wash it off my skin
along the running water
then i'll go to bed
hoping to wake up
with a full heart
the next morning

∞ Broken Wings

☾

this is my last trial
just that my heart
keeps urging me
but i can break it
no more for none
it's been shattered
into pieces all around

- I'm sorry that i'm not as strong as you thought i was
I'm not sorry that i tried to be for you

☾

everytime i think
of your voice
i swear i could hear
the sound of my heart
cracking in half
inside of my chest
all. over. again.

The day you stopped caring

☾

those times you
keep me hanging
they make my night
too hard to get through
and my heart race
too fast to catch you

« False Hope

☾

you say you're here
but for how long really
for how long until
you leave again and
i'm left with nothing
but a broken heart
and dried tears.
you're acting as if
nothing happened,
as if we've never been
through this scenario
a hundred times before
but i promise that if
i fall asleep crying tonight
i will let go of my heart
to come with you.
it never wanted me
since the beginning
either way

◄◄ Rewind

☾

i'm not sick
just a crushed heart
and a lost soul …
and i keep begging
the ones who don't care
about the harm
they've done in leaving
to give a damn about me

3:26 am

☽

i don't understand
how you expect me
to make you feel
complete when
i'm still looking
for the   pieces
i   left   scattered
        behind   on   the
    path   i   took
to   earn
you

                = Scattered

☾

why people who
are meant
to be
so close
are
so far
away

... Distance

☾

it's only been
a month
three weeks
six days
forty minutes
fifty-one seconds
and twenty-seven
unread texts from him
and i can't see the world
the same way anymore

Changing …

☾

there are so many things
that i want to say
if i just knew
how to start
…

Unnamed

☾

the more i'm hurt
the colder i get
you cause the damage
so you pay the cost

Unhuman

☾

i'm tired of waking up
every single morning
living in the fantasy
that you'd be rolled
in bed beside me
to find emptiness
laying on my white sheets

Ø Empty

☾

don't you dare and say you're ready
to give up everything for me
when you don't even see
the meaning of "everything" in love

- **love** is about risking it all

☾

i knew i was surely
lost in your love
when you left and
i kept the door open
waiting for you
to come back

when will you come home

‐·‐·‐·‐·‐·‐·‐·‐·‐·‐·‐·‐·‐·‐

☾

you know what you did
is wrong and shameful
when you're telling
the story of what happened
and you counterfeit yourself
as the one being done wrong
in spite of the fighting guilt
holding your tongue back

- Vague Lies

sometimes i just feel
like taking a long break

not from you ...
from the world

<< Breath

☾

i just wanted to be strong
so i can cope with your absence
i didn't know that with strength
comes thorough negligence
now even those close to me
have to suffer from the
effect of your absence, too

● Abandoned Attention

℃

every day that goes by
without you in it
is poisoning my existence
all the bad feelings
are fattening inside me
growing bigger than
the size of my capacity
digging a hole in my chest
every day is eating me up
like a baleful cancer
steadily but deadly

♋   Cancer

i think i'll heal eventually
it just might take a while

-    Mourning

94

☾

the night he left, i dressed up in black
held my hair up in a ponytail
sprayed my body in a brand new perfume
and lit up a couple of yankee candles
in the smell of midsummer's night
then i sat in the bubble chair
viewing on the room balcony
and sipped my bitter coffee
as i watched the crimson light of dusk
being swallowed by a moonless sky

-     Funeral

☽

in times you let me down
i turned to dark chocolate
to sympathize with the swarthy tone
plucking the strings inside of me
music humanized in
my extremely hot tears
and with every bite i take
i question myself
   " how can it be
so sweet yet so dark"

        - Darkness in the taste of Sugar

☾

the bruises he leaves
from his hunger for me
look like the scars
i got from falling
when i was a kid

✤ Hickeys

New Moon

Moonlight Whispers

☽

☾

you're the beautiful mystery
that sets my curiosity on fire
beneath your gorgeous eyes
lie the secrets of life
i've ever-long yearned for.
on your luscious lips
rest the magical words
i've everly been chasing.

︿ Beautiful Mystery

☾

his smile, his eyes
got me falling in deep
hi voice, his laugh
got me dreaming far
his hugs, his kisses
got me wanting him
his words, his silence
got me going crazy
his touch, his smell
got me craving mercy
then i fancy the way
he looks at me
just as i relish the way
he holds me
and i slowly keep falling
in love with him

❖ Precious Color

☾

because just the thought of you
makes my heart explode like fireworks in the sky

✳   Firework

you make me strong
when you come close
only to take it all back
when you come closer

fi The Weakness of a Strength

☾

he had the most gorgeous eyes
washed blue like the waves
of a deep peaceful ocean
not the kind of oceans
that make you reaching
to debark your anchor
but the kind of ones
that make you wanting
to sink in …
to get lost in the depths
and so i did

⚓ Anchor

he planted a garden
in my deserted heart
within the touch of the night
he'd water it during the day
when the sunshine breaks in
through the curtains of the room
where we slept together
little did he know
that garden bloomed
under the moonlight

❀   Tropical White Morning Glory

☾

don't you get it?
i want all of you!
i said eagerly
my hands landing on his chest
my eyes still fully fixed in his
and my lips slowly nearing
he makes my modesty flow
with the running current
to the land of lost objects
right where my heart
lays gracefully auspicious

◀ ▶ All Of Me Wants All Of You

☾

i never believed
perfection existed
until i met you

#Flawless_Creature

☾

i know you're all mine now
but i still want more
i whispered in his ear
then stuffed my face
bach in his warm
muscular neck

" Whispers

☾

i met him and chose to stay
he makes me want to live
an entire eternity and yet…
still wonder if it'd ever be
     e n o u g h

Never Enough

☾

that night though
i looked closely and
saw my desire for him
burn on blistering fire
float into pieces of ashes
on the solid ground
and fly with the first
blow of autumn winds
flirting with the crispy leaves
of a late November afternoon

☭ Fallen Leaves

what attracts you to the sky
that you lift your eye up
every time there's no roof
above your head, he asked
it's the moon, i said
my soul keeps digging
for its light to sneak in
and enliven her like
you do to me

Moonlight Magic ☽

☾

just like the tides of the ocean
are bulged by the new moon
risen and fallen in one pull
your gravity drags me to you
to the moment i fell in love
with every inch and part of you

⟨⊙⟩ *gravity*

☾

… i love you …
i've loved you since the beginning
and i shall love you until eternity

∞ infinity

☾

we see the same moon
YOU and I …
and when we whisper
the light carries our heart wishes
to where they truly belong

→ Journeys & Destinations

and then i figured
i might just be a moonchild
drawn to the moon in a way
that cannot be explained
in simple ordinary words
living in an absolute fantasy
that cannot be permeated
finding pleasure in dancing
under the lunar light
and measuring my days
with the different phases
i might just be a moonchild
passionate of the moon
where i shall belong ..
to whom i ever belong

' Moonchild

☾

i want to be as faithful to him
as the wolf of mellow woods
　　　t h a t
every night of a full moon
races to the top of the hill
and howls in such a whim
for the moon to notice her
sincere feelings of fondness »

☾

i loved you to the moon
and when i believed
that the distance back
was too short for a proof
i started seeking a way
that will take me higher

♥ I love you to the moon and beyond

☾

stars twinkling brightly
in the glassy dark sky
diamonds dazzling vividly
on the neutral background
sun rays gleaming intensely
way in the room and round
and for everything that glows
i shall favor you my treasure

✳   Glint and Glisten

☾

… then i woke up one day
and i was in total harmony
in harmony with myself
and what's around me
in harmony
with what i went through
with who i chose to be
and what's waiting for me

♀   Heavenly Earth

what's so special
about him
that had you
choose him
over the big
wide world?
they asked
him !
i said

It's just that simple

(

i can't explain
how it works
when i'm with you
but …
my soul gets jealous
sharing you with
my own body

0 Love is Selfish

☾

i never knew the
taste of love until you
and now i'm wondering
how was i alive starving
this whole long time

Silent Echoes

won't you lay your
head on my chest
maybe then
you will believe it
when i tell you
that my heart beats
way faster for you

The Pulse

☾

i don't want to ever
see a day i regret
living without you

Skyline

☾

your touch filters in my skin
like does the water in the clay
your kiss enlivens my heart
like does oxygen to my lungs
and every other small trace
you leave behind ...
finds its way into my soul

Depths

☾

i think i need a map
i lost myself in his smile

* Wanderer

☾

i can't give a reason
why i should leave him
but i can give a billion more
why i should stay and love him

❀ ❀ Aloha

☾

kiss me
so hard
i forget
the past
i had
lived
without
you
in

❚ Rebirth

i'm brave
i'm strong
i'm unbreakable
and unforeseen
i'm everything
i choose to be
until his eyes
fall on me

☪ Surrender

and if i leave
everything behind
and run to you today
will you be waiting
on the other side
with open arms

- Runaway With You

☾

most people spend a lifetime
looking for the right one
and sometimes fall on
the wrong choice
i feel so lucky that
i found you when
i wasn't even looking
and it just couldn't be
any more perfect
than this

　　… Soulmate …

forget about
internet, alcohol
and drugs
i'm only addicted
to you

Hooked

promise me that
you'll always and
forever be mine
hold my hand
when i'm lost
hug me tight
when i'm cold
and save me
when i'm
drowning

Promise me that you'll
… Stay …

☾

i still think of
that dreamy night
everynight …
our hearts, connected
our breaths, intersected
our fingers, intertwined
our skins, brushing
our lips, colliding
our bodies, eclipsing
and the lust of life
present in the specter
of our pure sacred love

- Sacred Love

☾

to all the exes
he ever had:
thank you for
leaving him so
he can be mine
he's everything
i wished for

✉ Misty Notes

☾

i don't know ..
there's something
about him that
makes me smile
unconsciously

✳ Angelic Soul

☾

legends have it that
he showered with the dew at night
dried himself under the moonlight
and dressed in a starry sight

◆ Dream Knight

☾

to his mom and dad:
thank you for giving birth
to the purest and most ravishing
creature on planet earth
but most of all
thank you for
letting me
steal him

✉ Crystal Notes

☾

it was very late at night
i was dancing in the rain
with the heels in my hand
laughing out gratuitously.
till you came and took me home
held my hand as you drove
sneaked admiring peaks at me asleep.
i heard the car stop by somewhere
i felt you unbuckling me, was half awake
you put your arms around me
lifted me up gently
and walked us into a room
that smelled in my perfume
rested me on my bed slowly so that
my body had touched the soft sheets
underneath my bold golden dress
you pulled the covers and tucked me in lovably
before you turned off the lamp nearby my bed
i felt a kiss landing breezily on my forehead
and thought it was farewell
as you walked away ...
i grabbed your hand and whispered stay
you looked at me and grinned an eternal smile
and the rest is known under the secrets of night

-     Erotic Infatuation

☾

if life was a book
you'd be my favorite page

❧ Fluorescent Ink

the way he looks at me
gives me butterflies.
they make me blush
like the rosy aurora
of north pole that
leisurely and comely
fade into the atmosphere

✳ Aurora

((

- i just want you to love me,
  and treat me as your most
  precious gift,
  my voice fainted
  that's all i ever asked for
  and never wanted more
- are you saying that i
  didn't love you enough?
  he inferred quickly
- love is not something you did
  it is something you do, have done
  and will always continue to do

  he kissed my lips passionately

' Random Quotations '

142

☾

once upon a time
we were living in a realm
upon the heart of helm
you were the prince
i was the princess
our love was a beautiful
flourishing royal story
of a heir who chose
to abandon her throne
and take off her crown
just so to be with you
build an empire brand new

♔ Spiritual Dynasty

☾

i surrounded him with my arms
like is wrapped the valuable gift
and maybe he was my gift
from the blessed sky
a gift i felt thankful to call mine
i loved him ceaselessly like the tides
constantly like the moon
and i was defiant enough
to tell the world about my passion
for a passion is not
something to be ashamed of
he was my muse
my desire
my whim

Blessed Gift

☾

that sweet taste of you
is decaying my existence
shifting it to an
obsession

☩ In the Flavor of Candy

☾

take me back
to the day
i met him
he stole my heart
and never gave it
back again

Young Love

☾

i wasn't sure before
but then you smiled
and i knew that
i was meant
to be yours

Those mornings waking up on your smile <3

☾

i'd been going down the sky
scattering around like a feather
thought i could go up high
instead i swept way farther
i watched the blaze of color
burning up the broad horizon
the sun ringing it like a collar
and a dark layer began risin'
i saw him hugging me into peace
till my old strain set about to cease

⟨ Gloaming

☾

at the end of the day
we remain but lovers
in the galaxy of fairy tales
perhaps what makes us
different and special
is that we dared to
reach out further and
touch the real world
proved that magic exists
that WE ... exist

✭ Legacy

☾

i had a dream
we lived in a house
on the moon and
were immortal

Moon House

☾

and i swear
i've detected the
reflection of stars
in his eyes

-    Mirrors

☽

i met happiness on your lips
Vanilla Life +

☾

the glorious enchantment
of seasons changing
collapsing one into another
some growing, some fading
all mixing within a holy elixir
but you... remain my favorite season

-     Marvel

((

it takes me back to
the time i fell for you
i was that golden crunchy leaf
floating down in the crispy air
and dancing along with the
lenient chill gust of stellar wind

&. Autumn

☾

in the midst of a frosty cold winter night
i felt warm ...

❅ When i'm with you

☾

he does to me
what the spring sky
does to the trees
when it awakens
the spirit of blossoms
with the pollination of bees

❀ Cherry Blossom

when it's storming outside
i lay in his arms
and close my eyes
he takes me back to
the sober summer nights
the hot beach days
lovely sandy picnics
and moist salty breeze
and when i open them again
the memory vanishes
but the feeling lasts

🛁 Tropical Paradise

(

dear moon
today
i love him
more than
yesterday
and the day
before
i'm loving him
everyday
even more
i think i'm sinking
slowly but surely

‡ Faraway

i was a rose in his hands
the more he loved me
the faster i sprouted
and so did i bloom
the less he cared
the easier i withered
and so did i perish

❀ Moonrose

☾

so i figured
you were the one
when my soul gracefully
perched on your heart
and found her home within you

- a stranger who became a lover

☾

i keep chasing
a glowing spark
in his eyes
to remember
the feeling
of being alive

☆ ★ Alive

（

ever since i met you
i've been seeing
rainbows and
butterflies
here and there

% *g*lamour

☾

all the dreams we never said
all the tears we ever had
we'll share it all hereby

�֎ Oath

with you entering my world
i learned some things :
i learned that love doesn't hurt
it's the wrong lovers that do
that we don't go around
hunting the "one" in the crown
the right one will eventually
stand out of the crowd
that sometimes we have to let go
of the questionably important person
to leave space for those more important for certain
i learned that love doesn't always remain
the same as when it has just started
but it's the ending that means everything
and there... my heart healed

✧ Golden Era

☽

quite often
i mistake you for an angel

-    or maybe you are

((

how can you be so avid ?
i've never secn someone
who loves as much as you do
or craves as bad as you do

Mundane

☾

i miss sleeping in your arms
and the sound of rain
cracking on the window
in the background of
your secret regards
and light touches
on my skin

◆ Honey Drops

☾

give me your hand
let us escape and
go somewhere
where the moon
hugs the tides
and the stars
giggle on the sides

★ The Shore

i remember once
i had wished
upon a shooting star
for eternal glory
and today
i got you

★ Sweet Glory

☾

i don’t get it…
something about him
makes everything
seem just right

ϟ Manifest Destiny

☾

when i say that
i'm obsessed with him
i actually mean that
my heart beats for him and
my lungs breathe for him
                as well

♥ Halo

i watched the sine
waves of the ocean
collapse in his eyes
and i found myself
floating on the
smooth surface
like a little seashell

◈ Pearl

☾

but if you get close
you might about hear
the ringing bells of
blood whistle in my veins
that... is what
your touch does to me
and if you knew
the pleasure of the feeling
you would never stop
touching me after

- Deft

☾

in the night
we were together
i felt like never before
i only felt ever full

Full Moon

☾

if he only knows
that before him
i was just an eclipse
dimming down the sky
and now i'm a new moon
lighting up the night

✧ Glow-up

☾

but when my heartbeats
are dressed in fear
you whisper in my ear
and it all calms down
together

☮ Safe Haven

☾

it's not because
you're my first
that you mean
to me the most
it's that you make me
feel so complete that
there's no more room
left for another
before or after

✓ Loaded

☾

even water
does not
irrigate
my thirst
like he does

♆ Saturated

☾

the moment
you walked into my life
with a piece of holy heaven
i wanted to grow old with you

❀ Leilani
" Heavenly Flower"

☽

the way you shine
the darkness in
my soul
even the sun
is jealous of

☀ Sunshine

☾

from the morning dawn
to the evening dusk
i'll wait for you
to come about
and invade
my life

🕐 Daily Horizon

☾

you know what could be
so pure and innocent ?
if we swipe up hearts
and swear to guard them
like when we guarded
our dearest own instead

-    Dusty Lavender

☾

and when he leaves my room
i look straight away at the moon
and ask when will i see him again

Berry Velvet

☾

you haven't just made
a difference in my life
you … have been it,
the difference

☯ Contrast

☾

the single spelling
of your unique name
kidnaps my mind
to wonderland
and cast it
in magic

◐ a Spell

just because i let you
pin my hands down
when we're making love
doesn't mean you can
hold them tight
when i refuse to do
as you ask

-    don't you know that i'm rebellious

((

he undressed me slowly
and looked in my eyes faintly
his hands pleasantly landing
on my exposed tiny waist
his peckish lips began approaching
" are you sure you want to do this? "
" i've spent a lifetime waiting
for this moment with you "
i responded at last decisively

❦ Virgin

☾

the tips of his fingers
slid down my skin
the moon complimented
what a beautiful sin

- Beautiful Sin

☾

i see you everywhere i go
on every face i see
even when i look
in the mirror
i see you !
tell me,
if this isn't love
then whose reflection is that

⁂ Patterns

☽

you changed my perception of masculinity, of humanity
♂ You

even when
we're falling apart
when frustration fills
the sphere between us
like acrid poison
you still give me
that passionate look
that reminds me of all the times
you pushed me against the wall
and held my hands up my head
as you kissed and tugged my lips
in a midnight rising crave

Temptation ..

((

no
it's not wrong
when our souls have mated for life
and we choose to link our bodies too
and take it beyond the spiritual level
no
it's not a mistake
to trade touches
that make our nights connected as one
the beginning and ending of everything right

♥ All under the name of love

((

the moment his lips
crashed on mine
made me salivate
for the rest of
the night

Salvation …

i had developed a shield
that grew not fragile
but stronger in the lead
though there are times
i let people in close
to the core of my being
even when it seems like
showing them the highway
to my conclusive weakness
all i held onto is faith
to make the one wise choice
but when they fail me and i break
i mend partially and keep on hoping
that someday some shot will make it right

- and that's how i met you

☾

i love the way you extract
the good in everything
exceptionally
the best in me

ひ Hidden Flair

☾

the way he makes me feel
can forever only be seen
in the split seconds when
my heart skips beats
my breath flees my lungs
and my cheeks bloom
like peachy pink lilies

Young Blood

☾

when we first met
i stayed up late
talking to the moon
moved by genuine innocence
i had started to feel
something new rising inside me
emitting in my veins
-   it's flowing during my sleep
giving me good peaceful dreams
and clotting under my skin in the full day
printing amiable soothing sentiments
-   tell me more
the moon seemed to enjoy the talk
-   he gives me that feeling
that nobody understands
when our eyes come across
my entire body ignites
and even when he leaves
it feels like he's still there
those sentiments he creates remain
it's strange but what's even stranger
it's not just him whom i like
i adore everything his touch scans
i've loved myself since the eve he hugged me in
he makes me appreciate the days
i live knowing he exists
on this planet
and i don't want just
a today and a now
with him ...

i want a forever
a happily ever after
am i becoming self-absorbed ?
what's wrong with me?
the moon chuckled secretly
- there's nothing wrong with you
it's just what love does
and it's in his DNA
- i don't get it
- you don't have to
but it's obvious
like blood on the snow

 Ago

☾

there's a whole universe
that beats inside me
i don't know how it started
but i know that the center of it
     i s   y o u

-    League

☾

you're not the only one
who can feed my hunger
you're the only one
that i'm hungry for

ॐ Lethal Sexiness

((

maybe you opened the doors for me
on a whole new world
or maybe you simply
opened my eyes
on the beauty in this world
either way
i'm so happy
to be able
to see again

🕊 Glimpse

((

wish i could live a thousand lives
and fall in love with the ocean
in every single life
like i fell in love
with the gorgeous
aqua blueness
merging in your eyes
and maybe once
in a lifetime
i will live by the beach
so whenever i miss you
i'll look at the wide ocean
stretching toward the endlessness
and remember that unmistakable
feeling I had when I met you

~ Thalassophile

((

love me like there are no feelings after
love me like there's no tomorrow later
love me like your entire life is counting on it
love me like you and i desire not as they permit
love me like the night has loved the stars
love me even when love leaves scars
and don't just love me herein when i'm whole
but also love me when all that's left of me is a soul

✿   Wishing on daisy petals

☾

ought they name me an astrophile
for loving the stars
ought they name a selenophile
for loving the moon
so maybe uranophile makes better sense
for i've loved them both
or perhaps they fairly must name me the Lover of Yours
for i've adored you
most of all

☽

Always & Forever

Made in the USA
San Bernardino, CA
03 January 2020